Trees are Life
Coloring Book to Save the Trees
Laurie Popp

Trees are Life

Coloring Book to Save the Trees

21 Drawings to Color

From Original Art from artist Laurie Popp

$1 will be donated to the Arbor Day Foundation for every book sold.

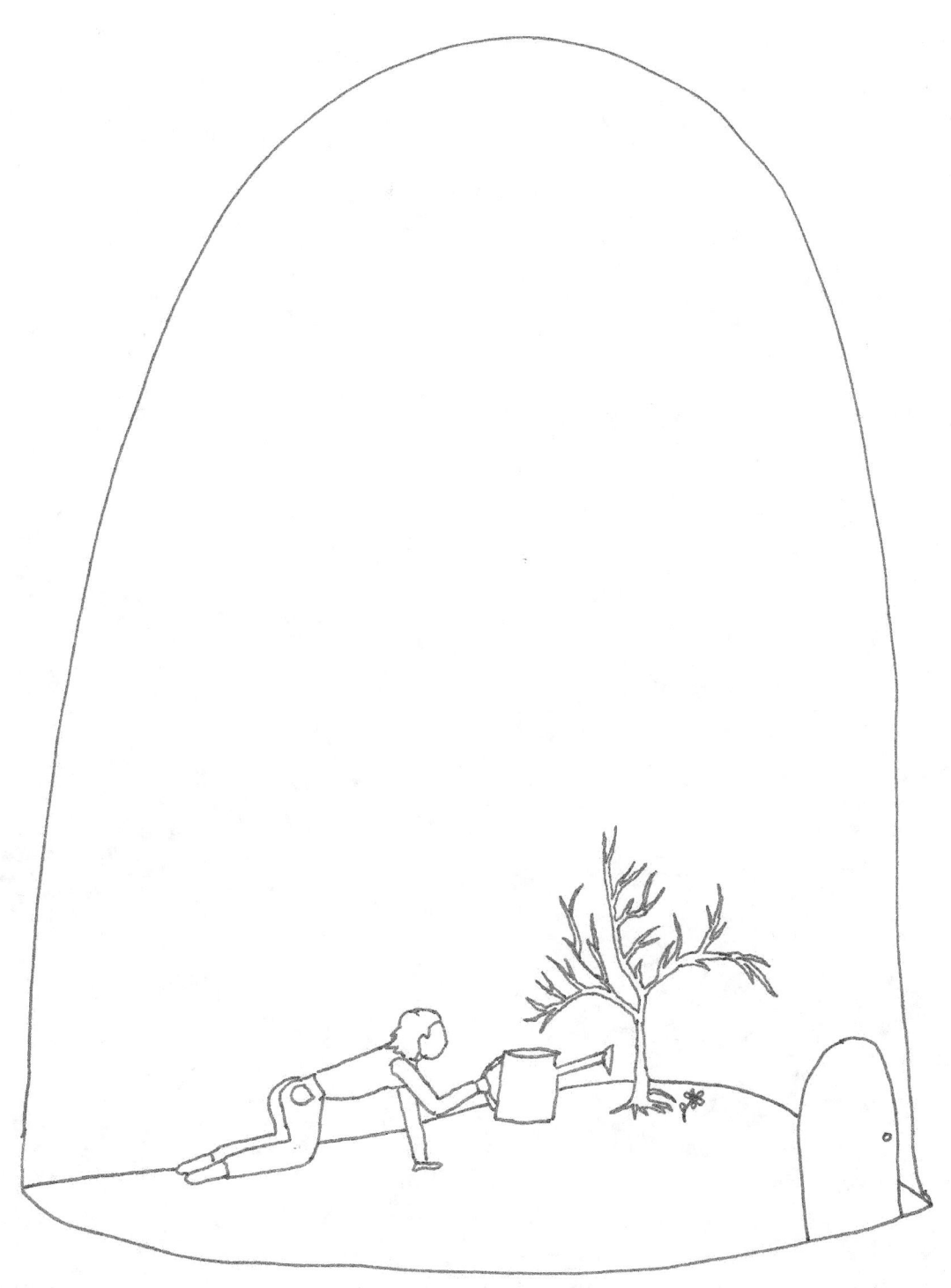

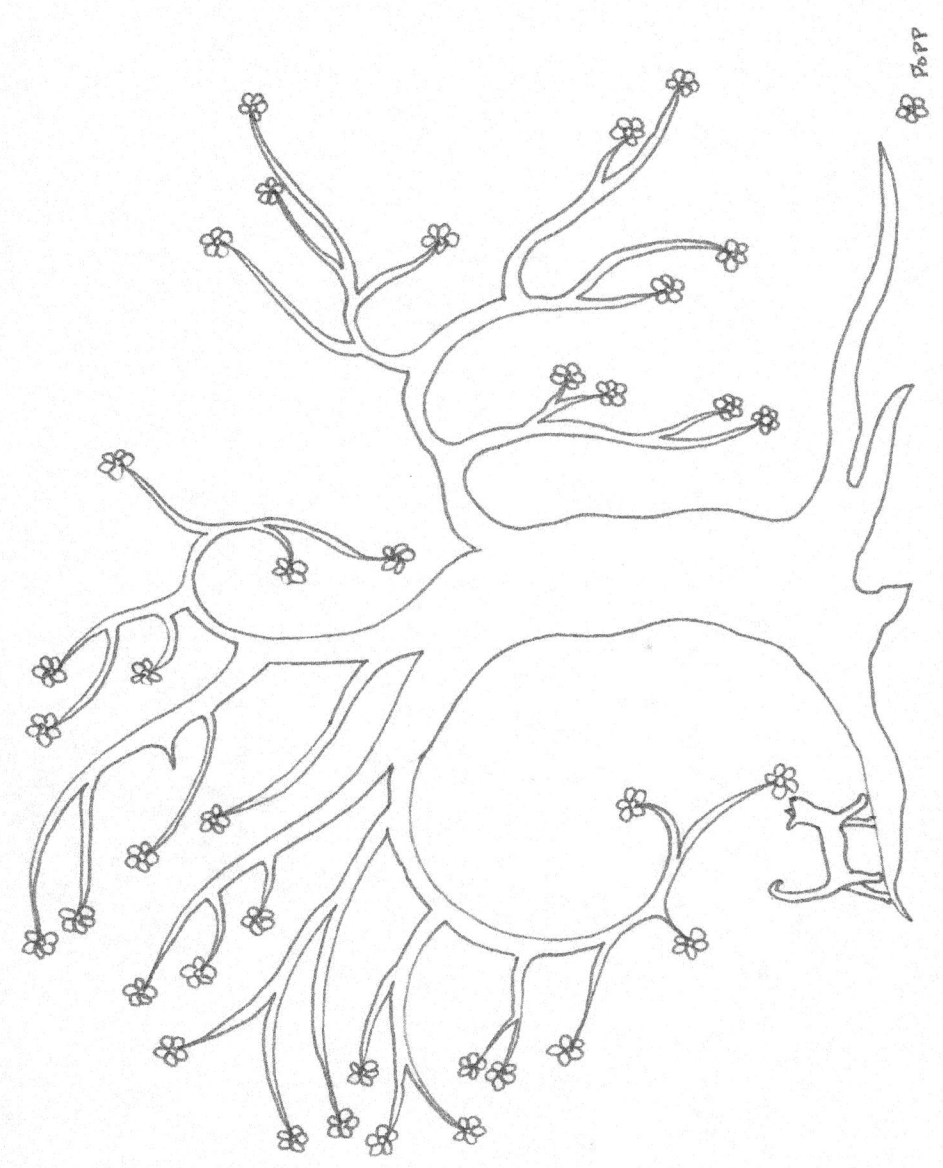

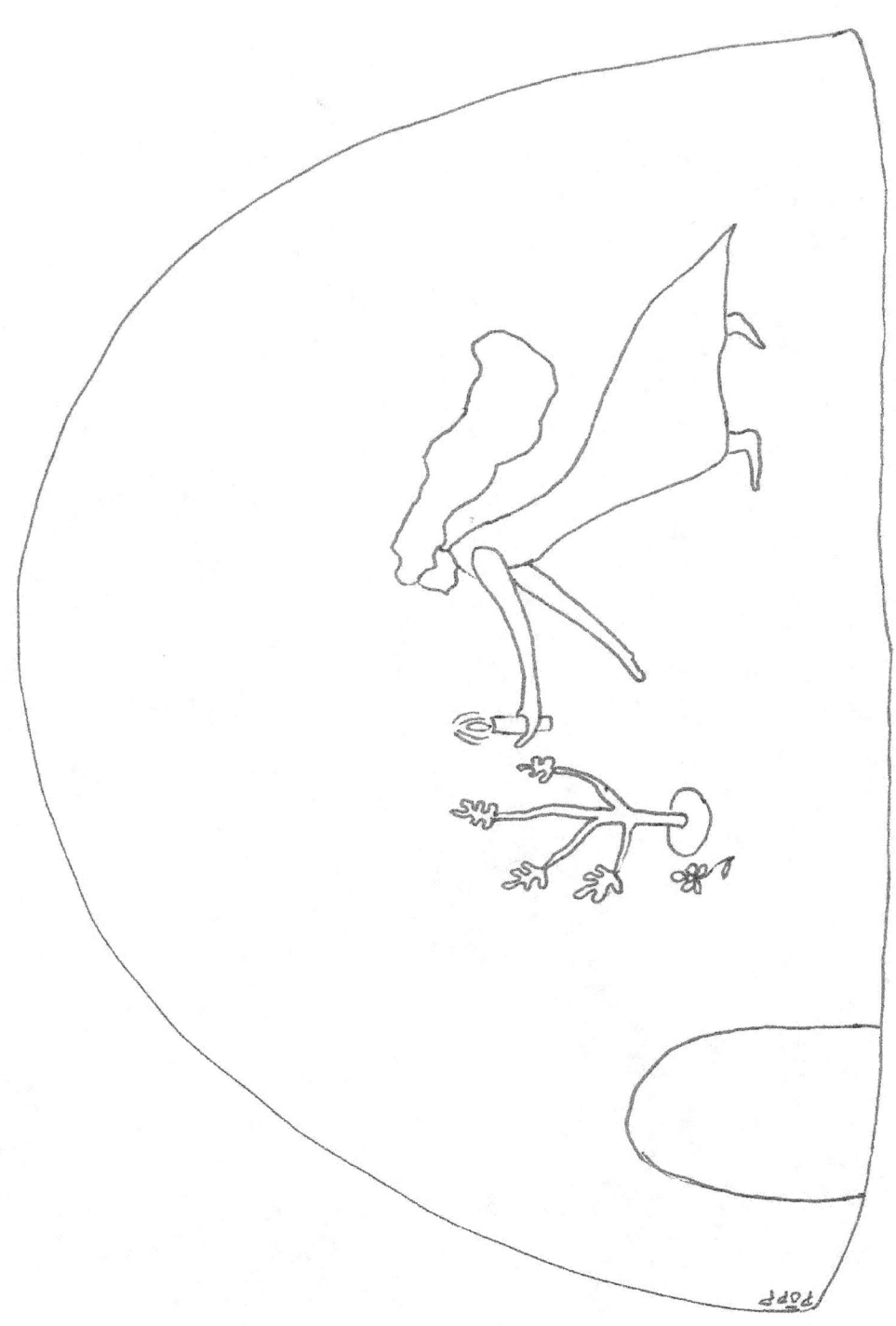

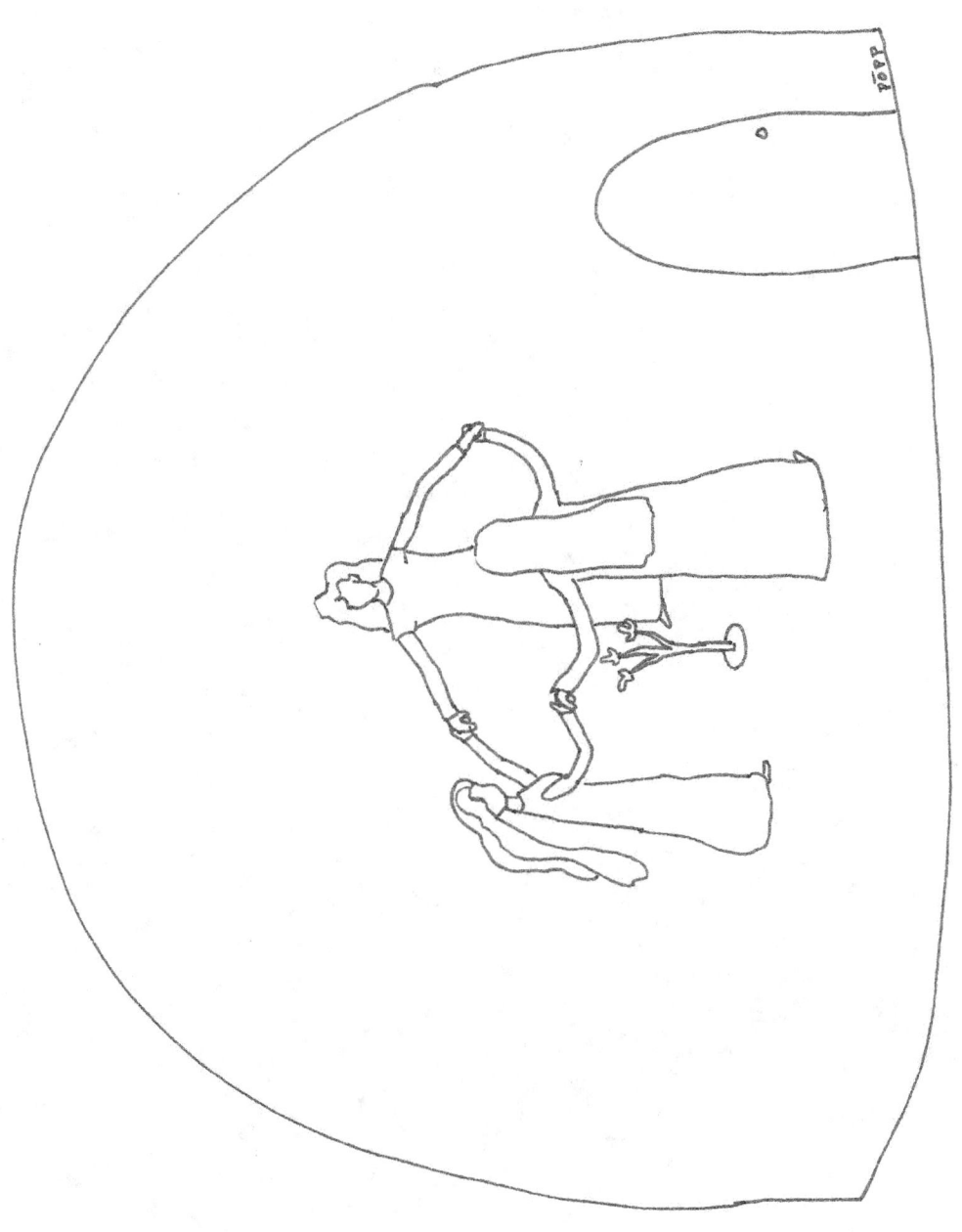

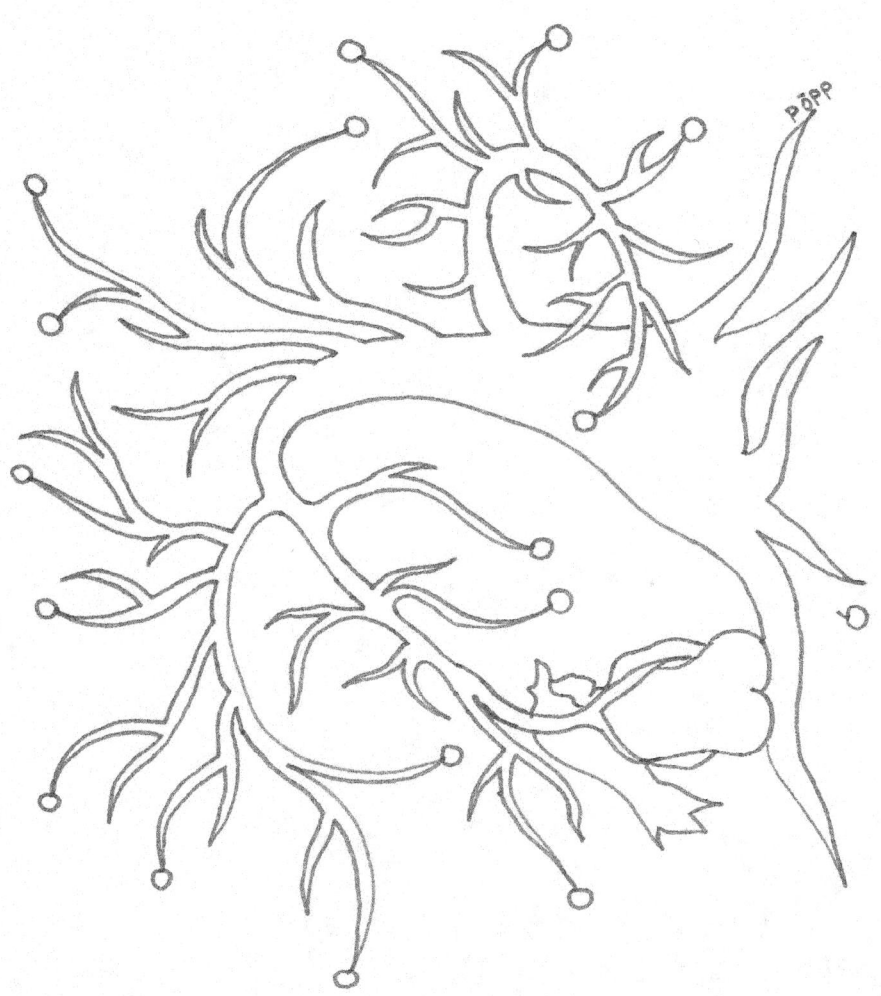

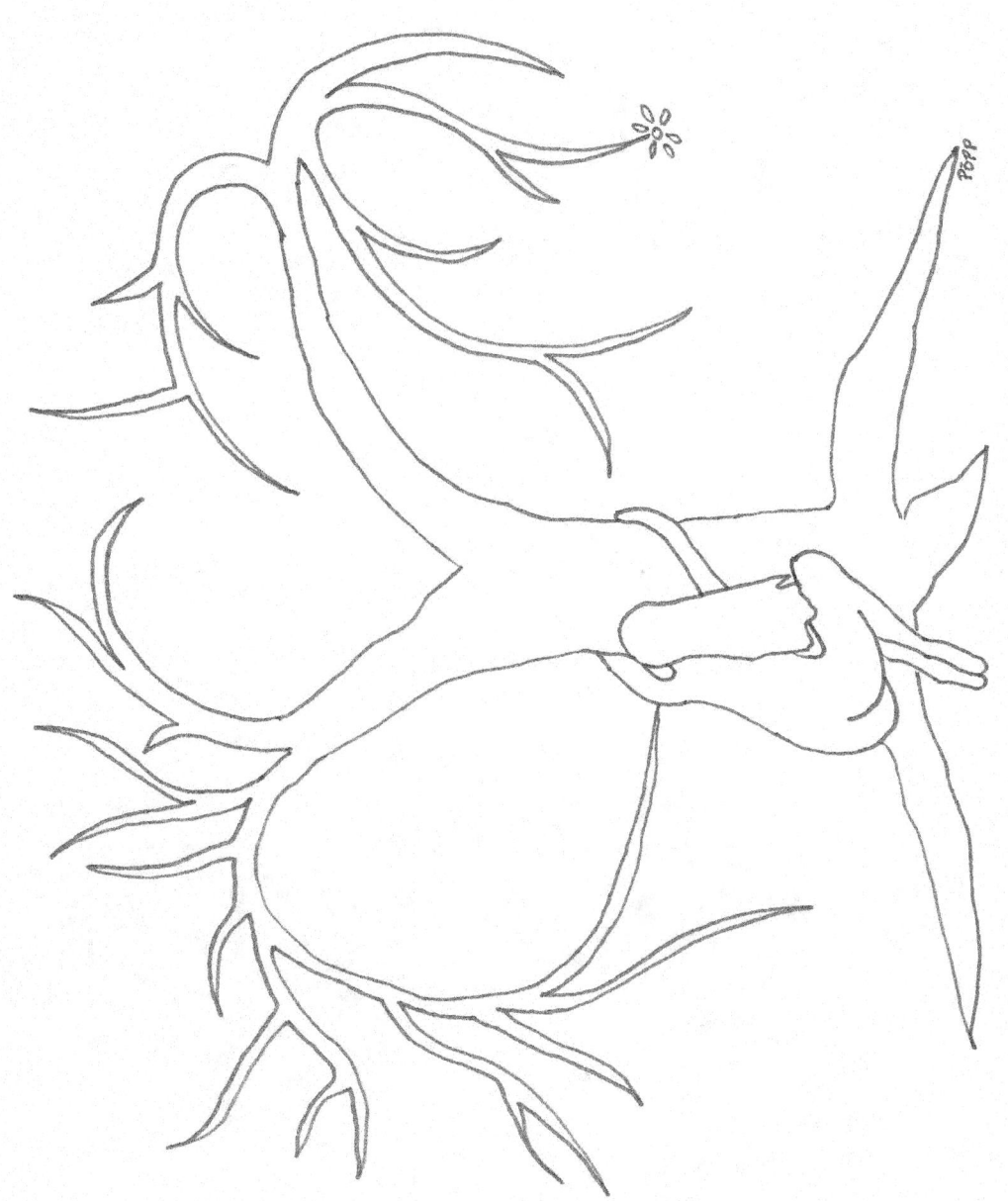

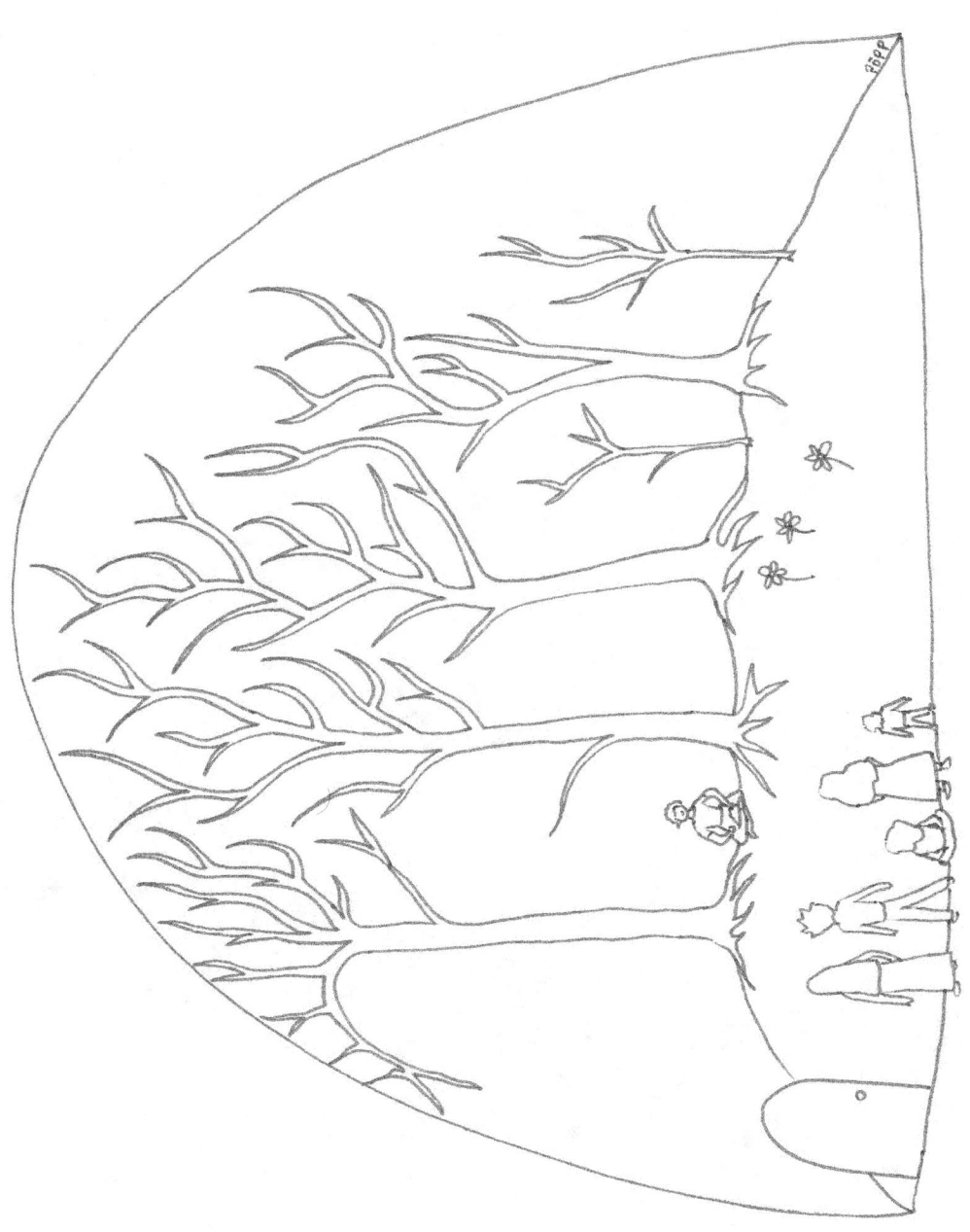

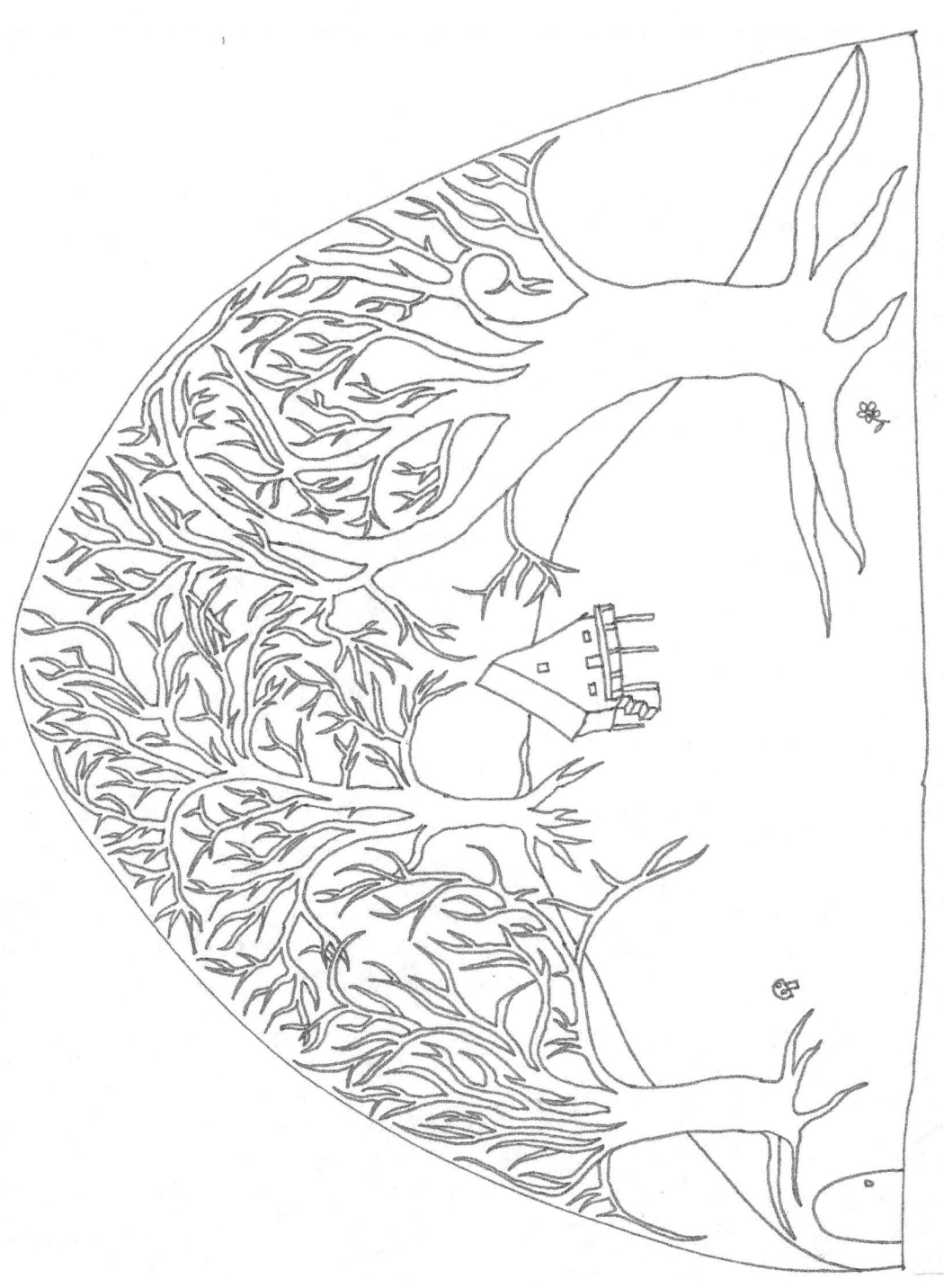

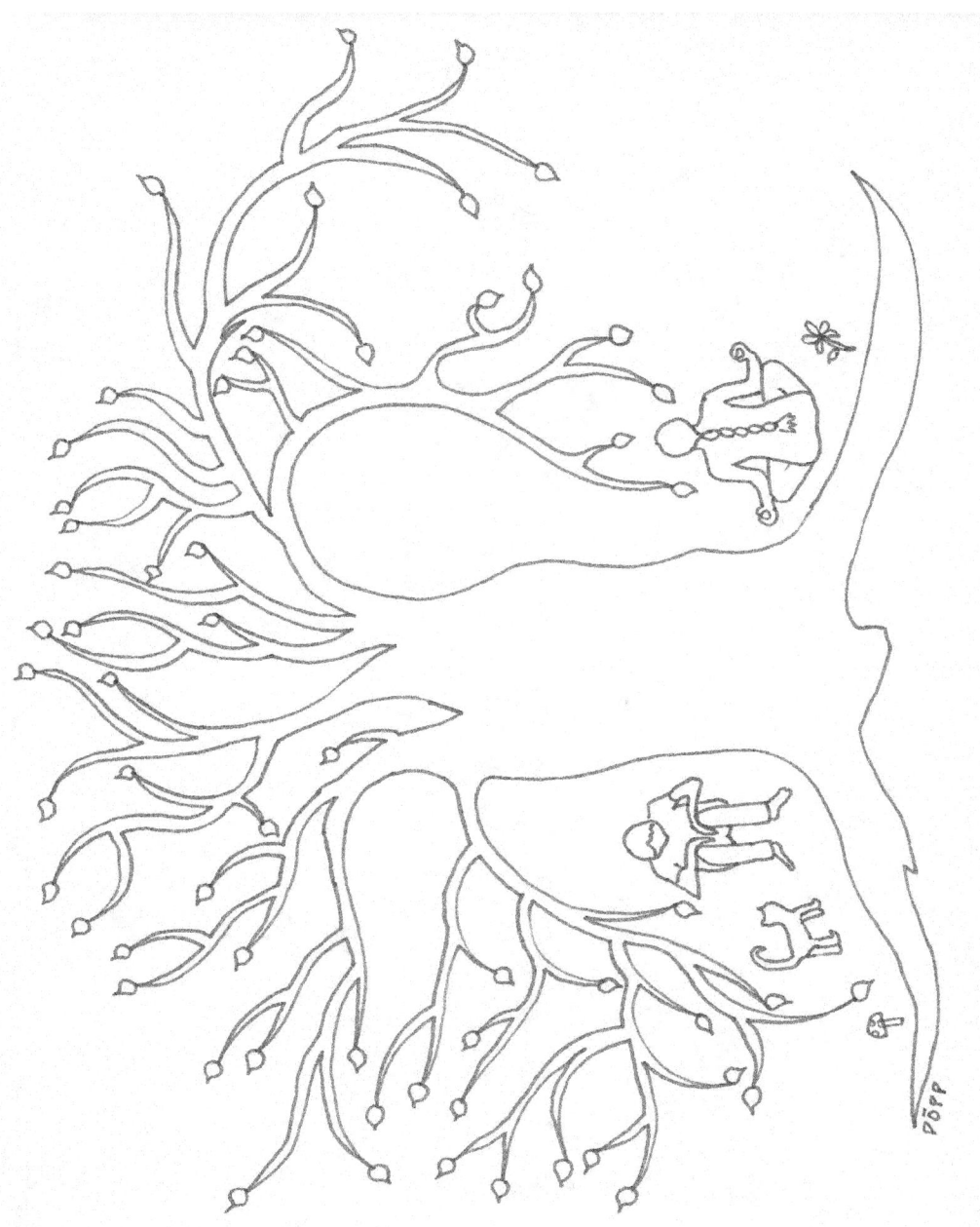

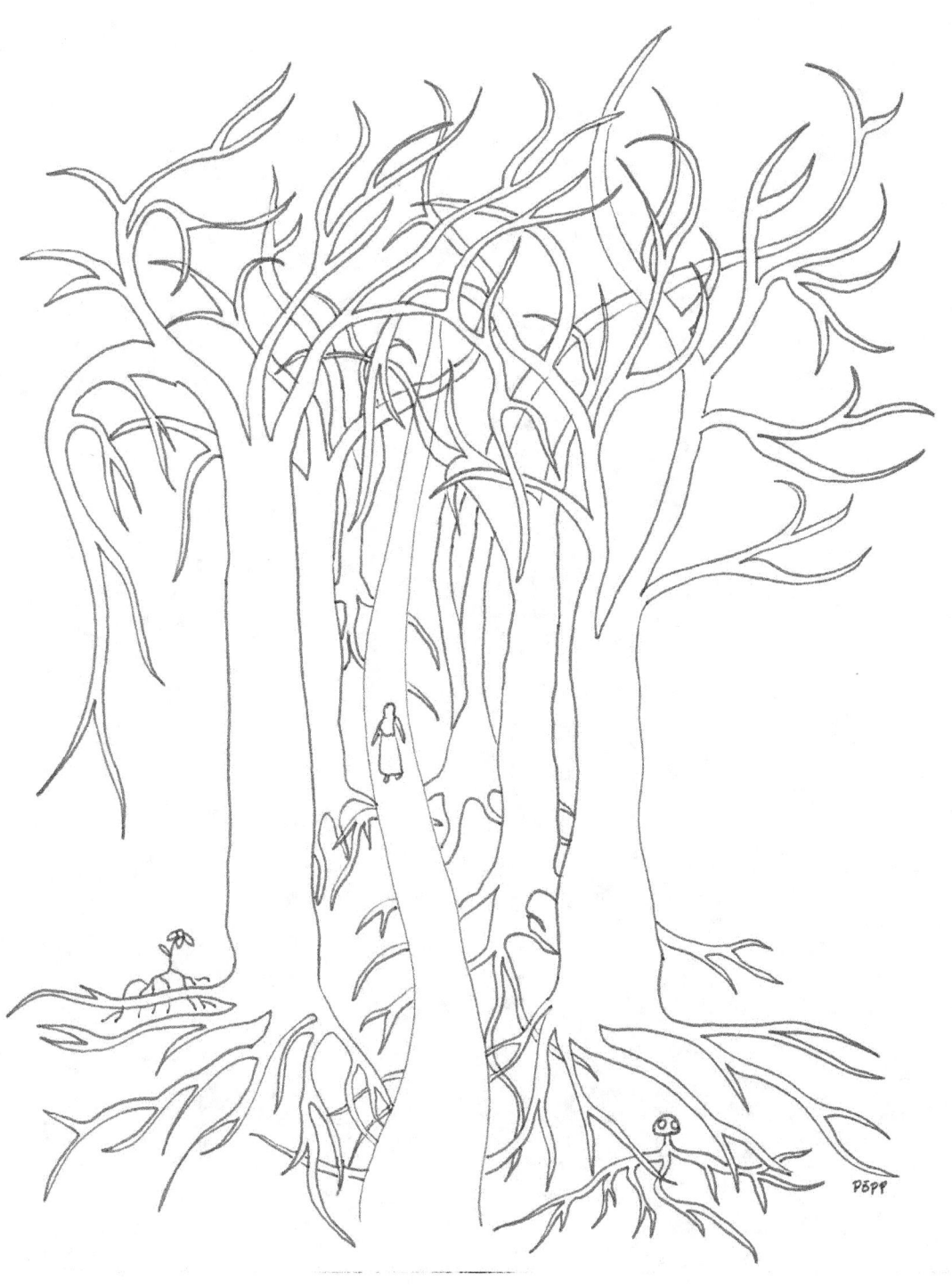

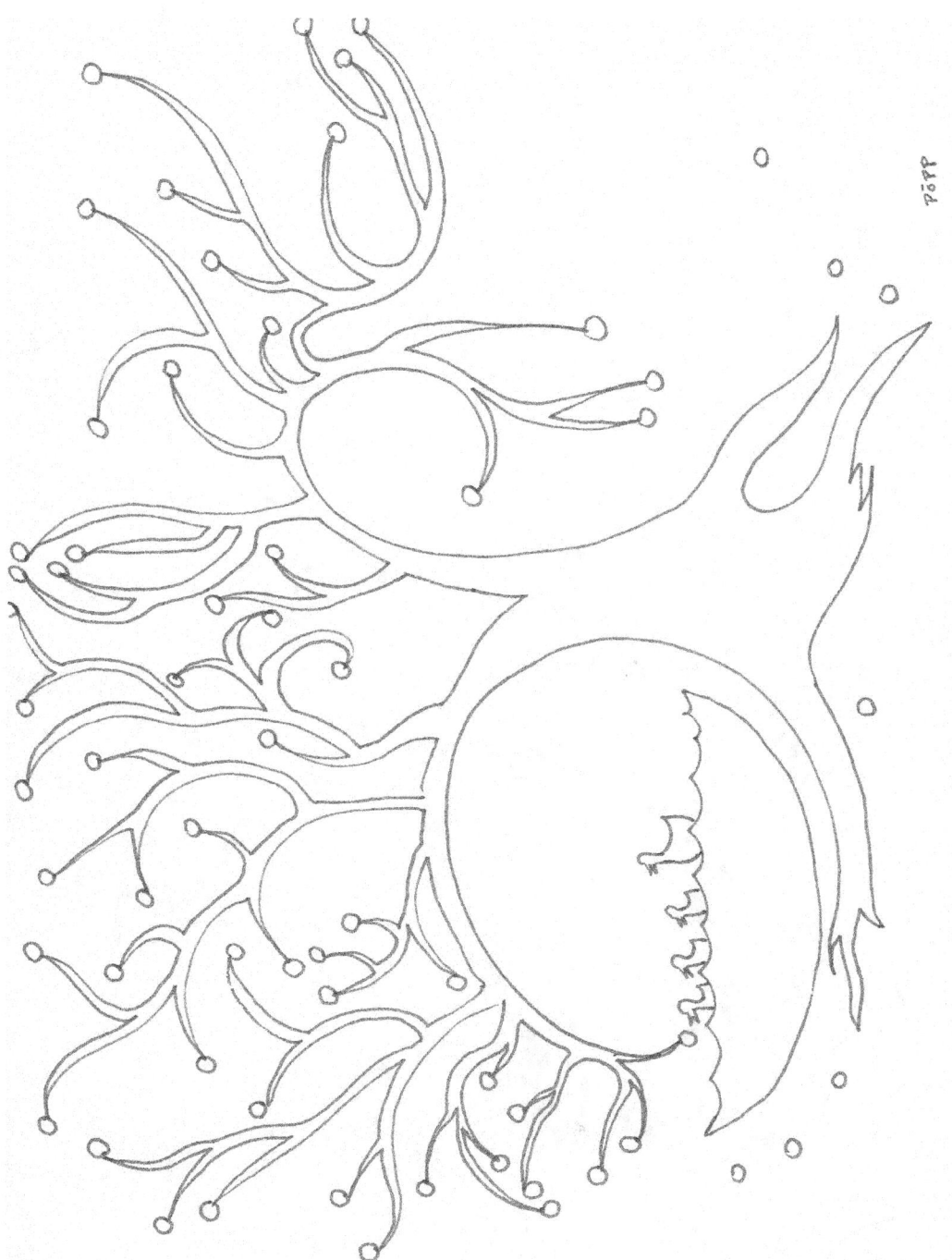

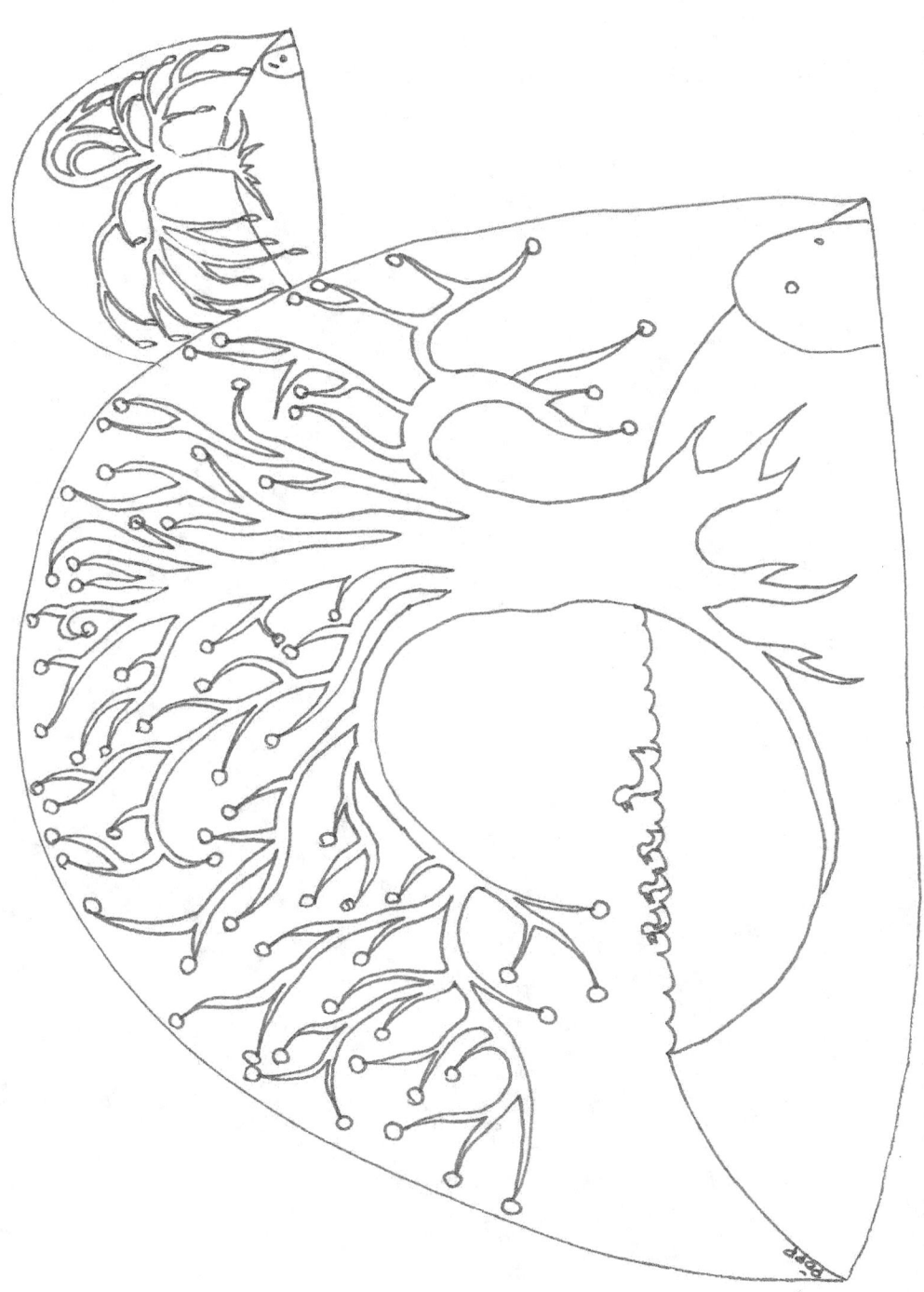

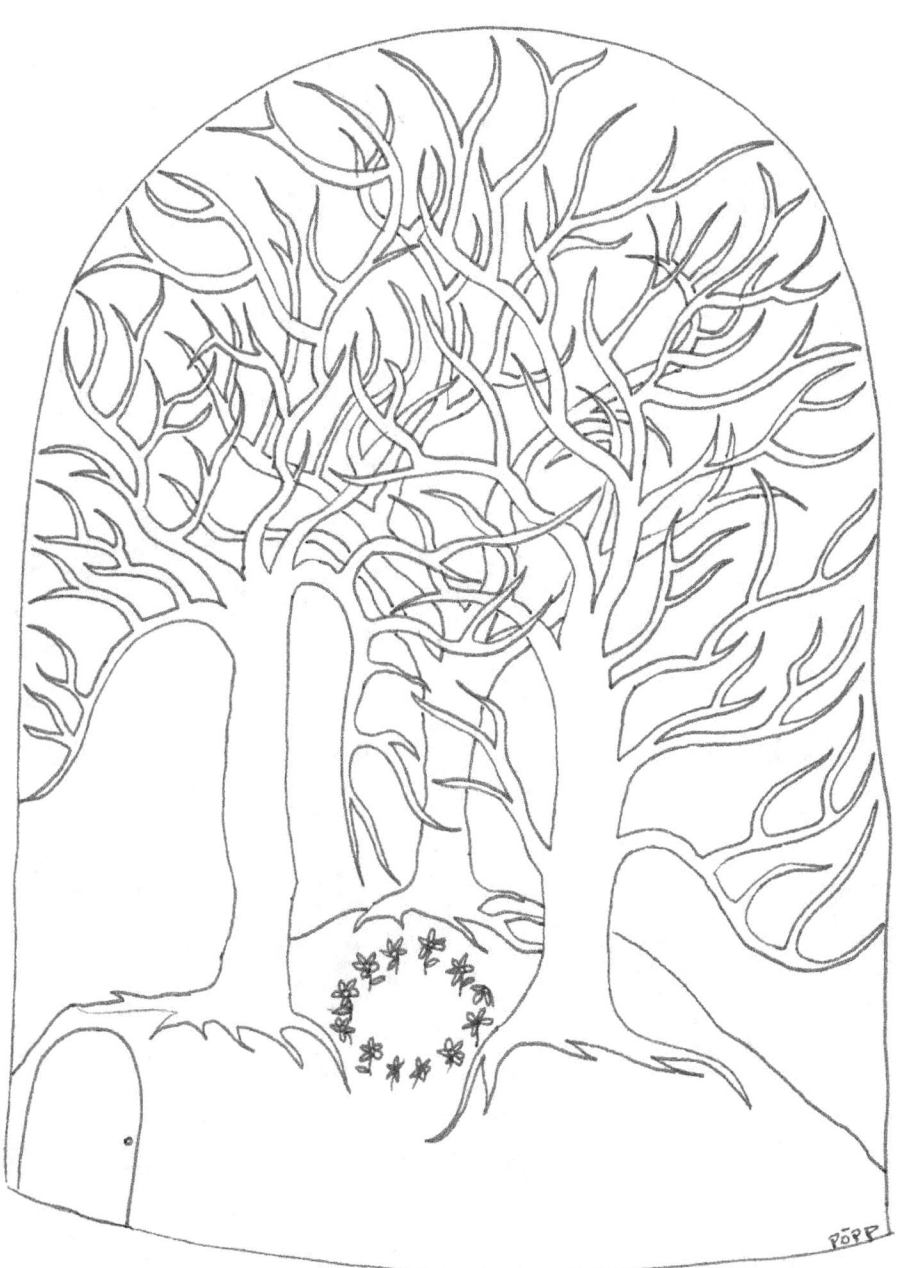

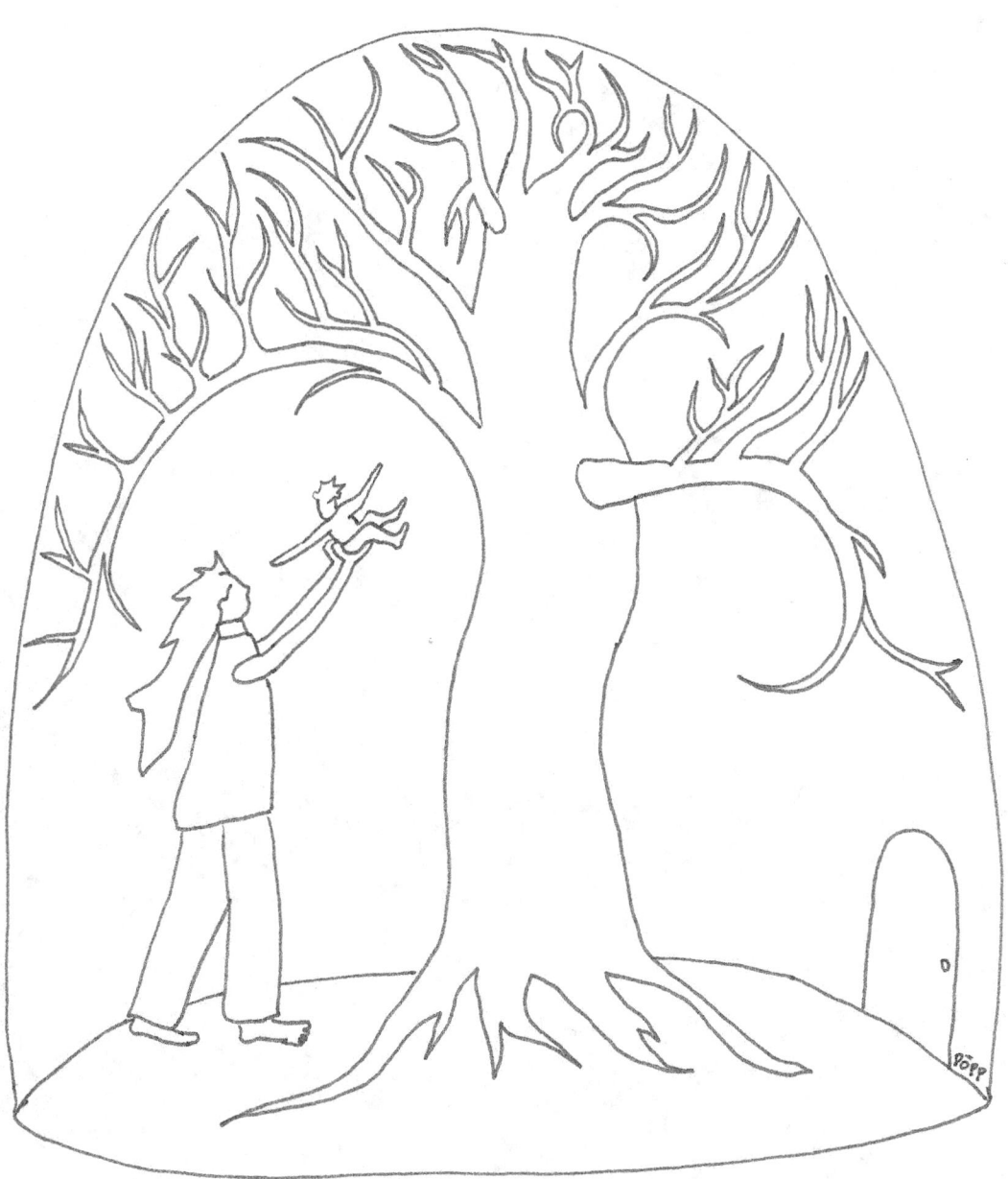

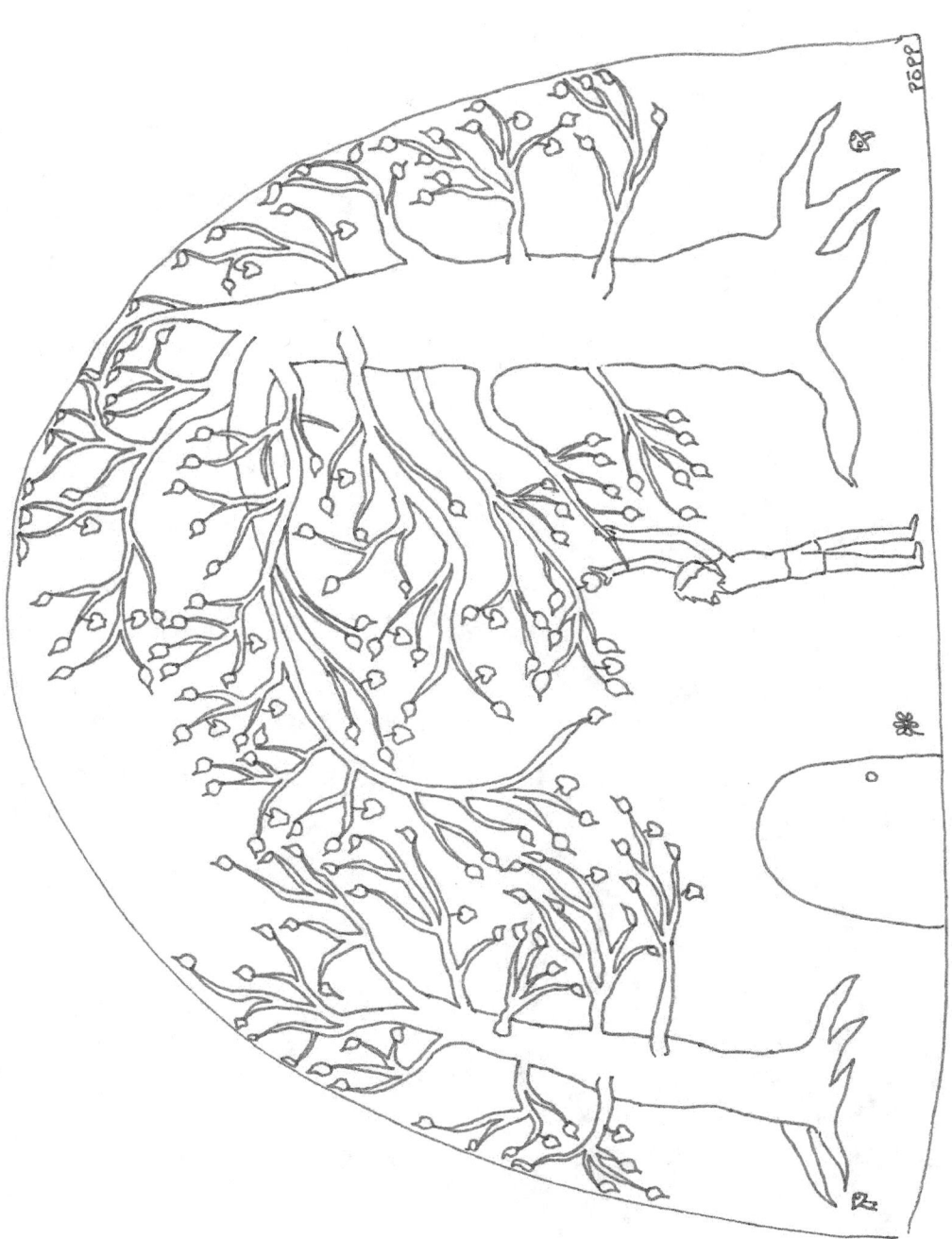

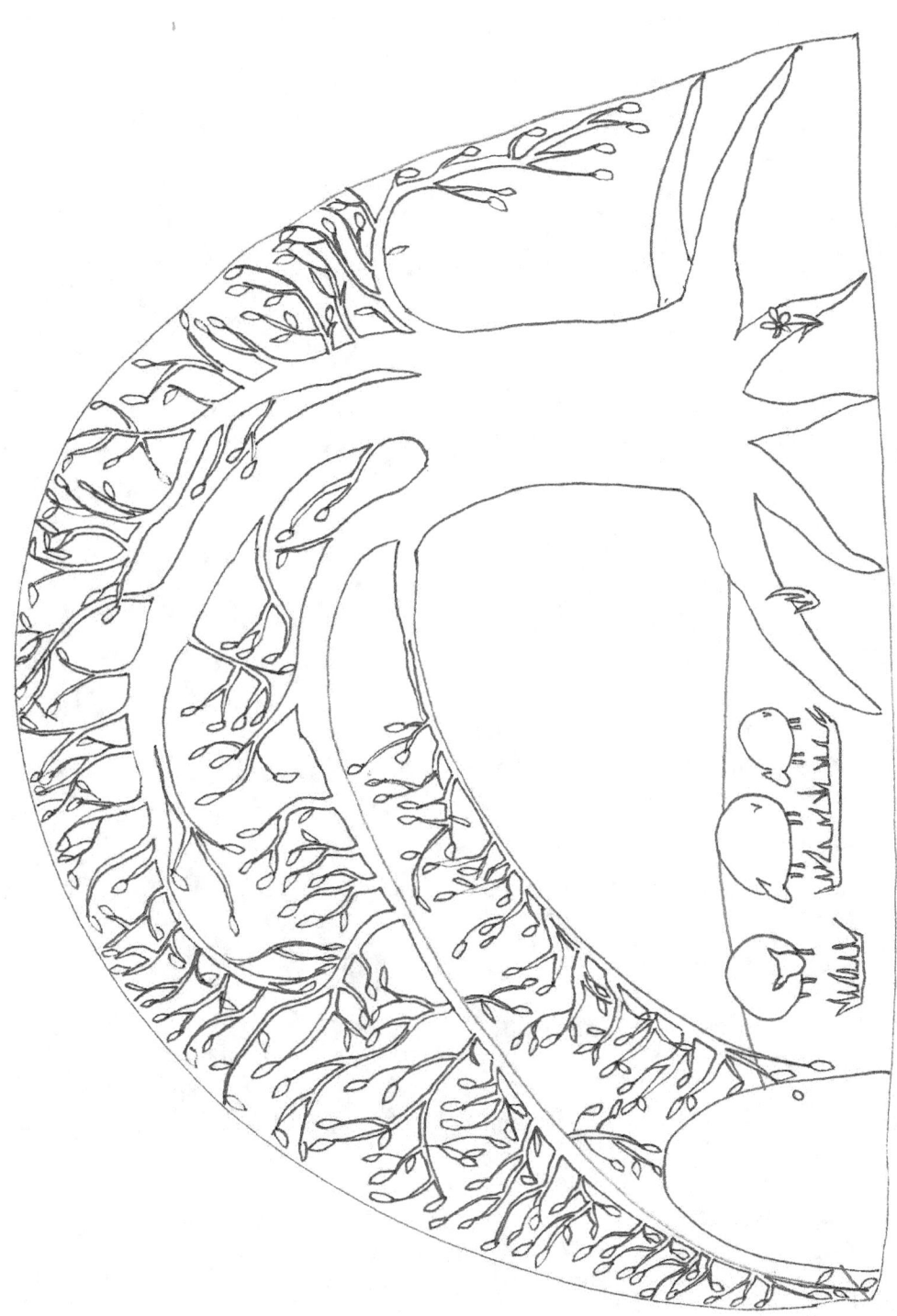

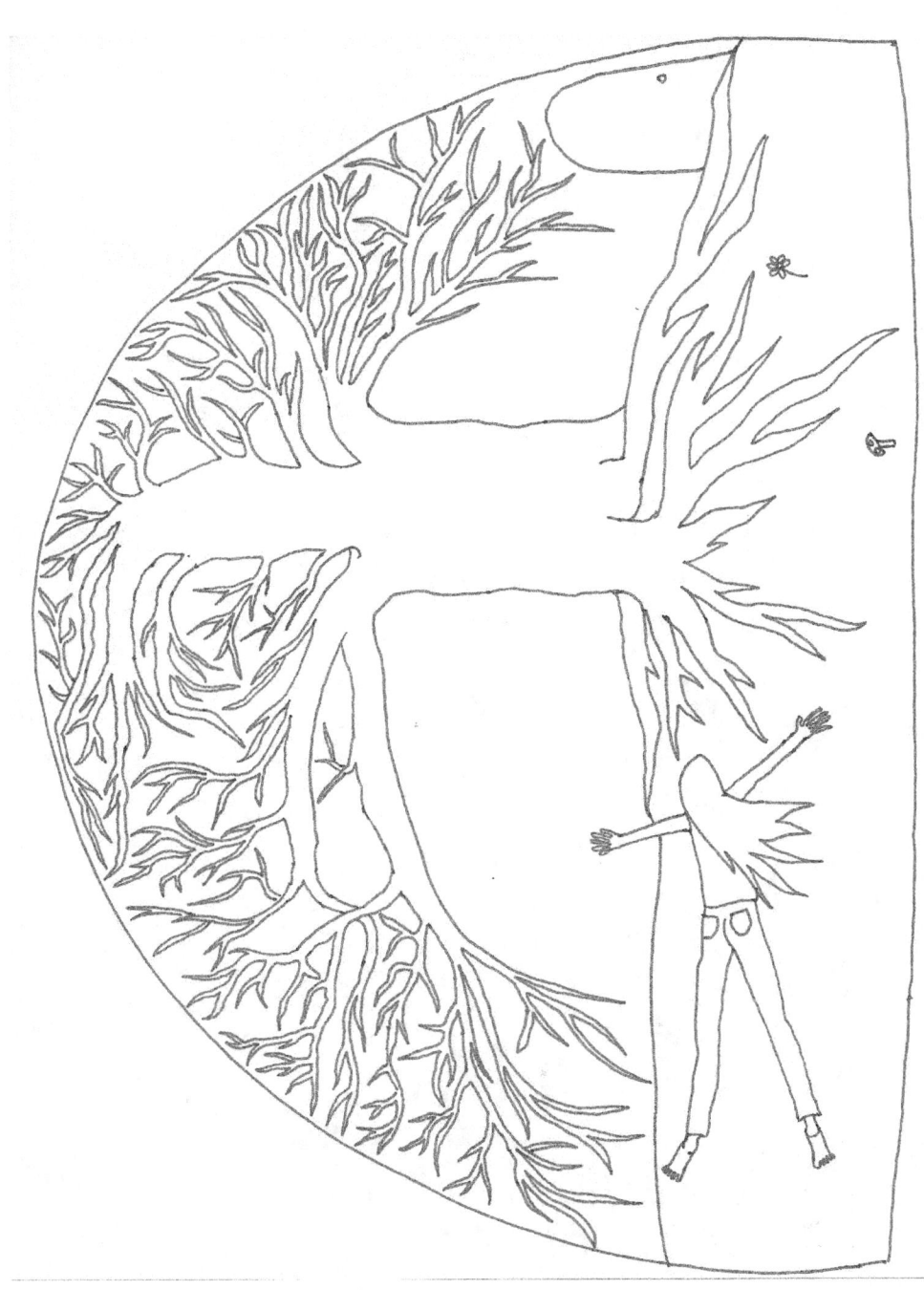

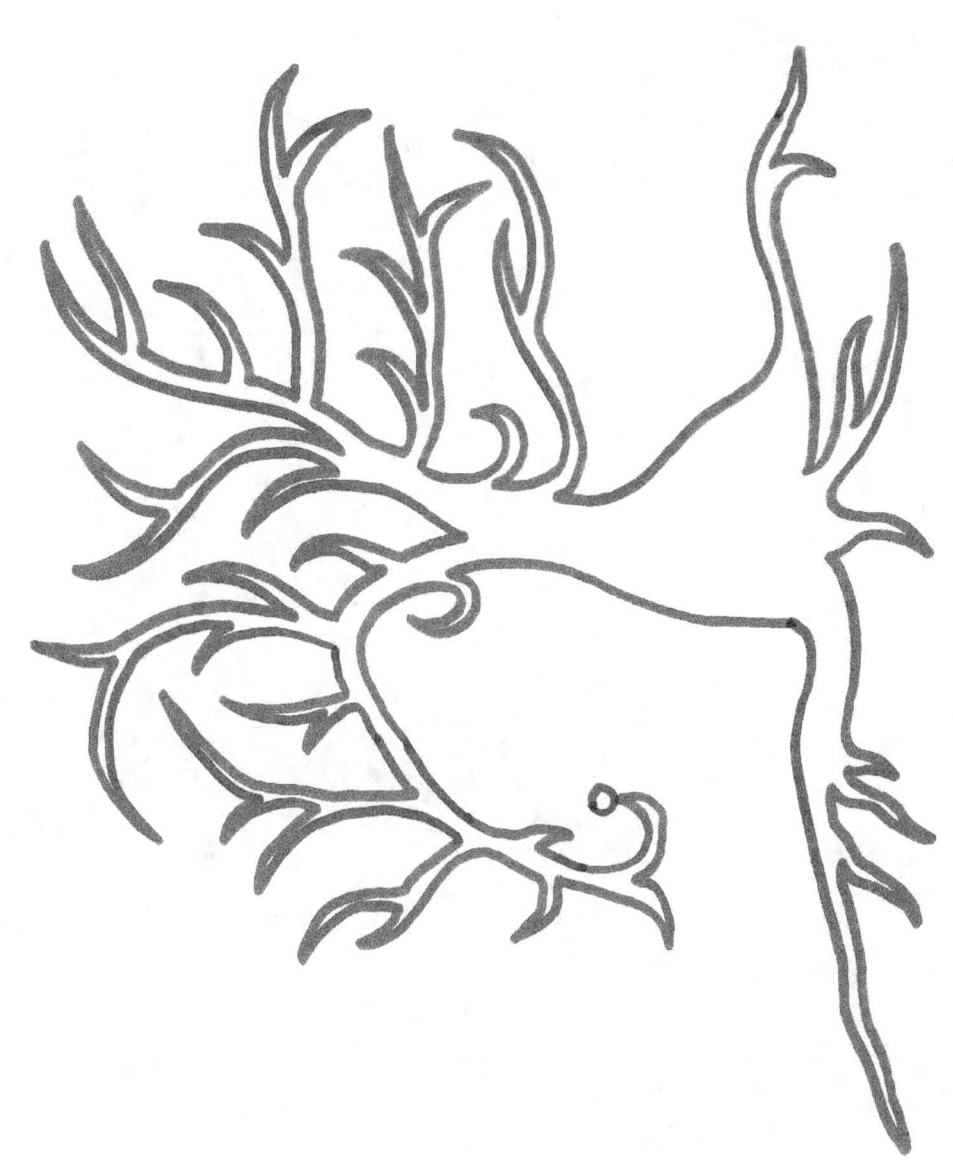

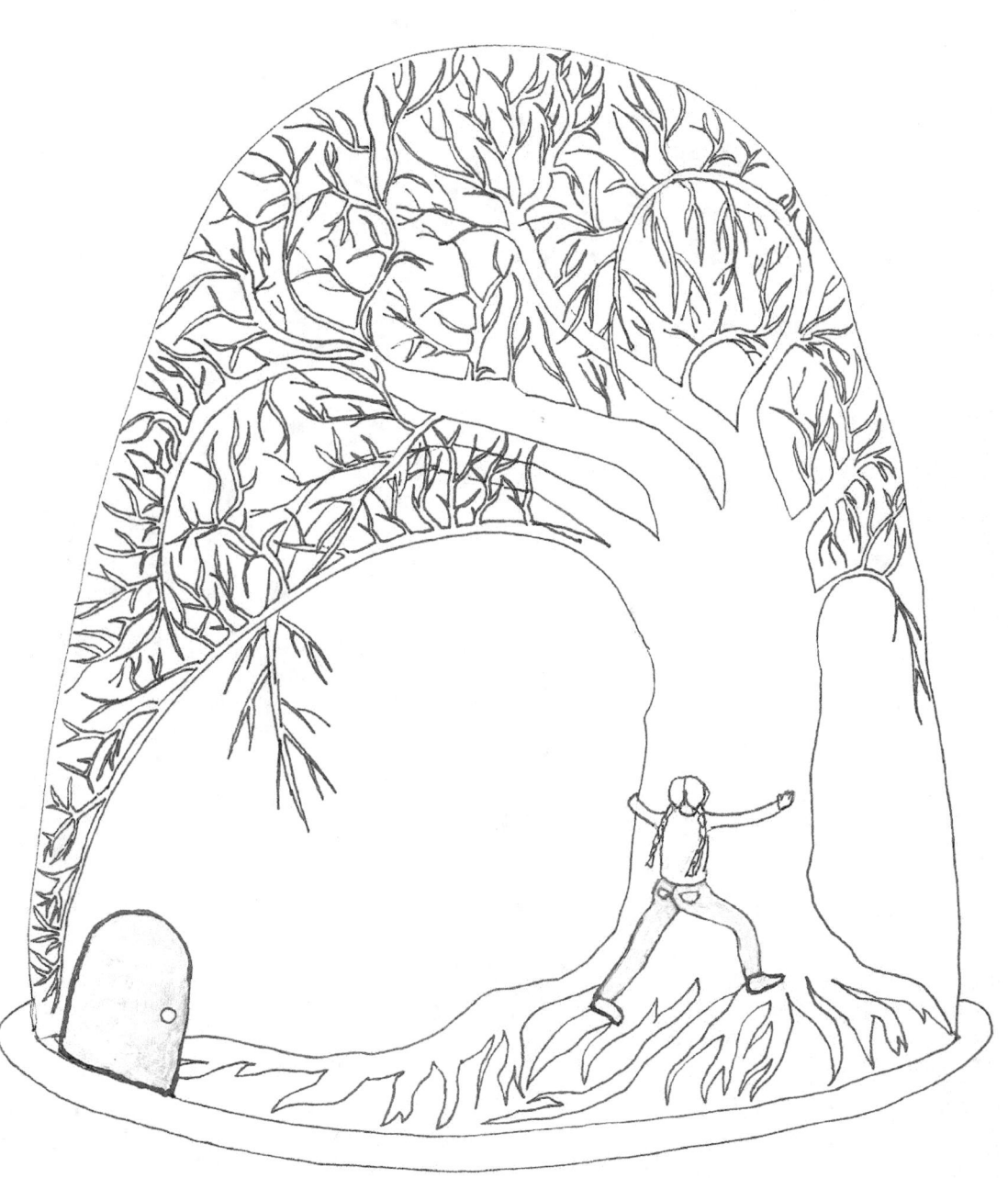

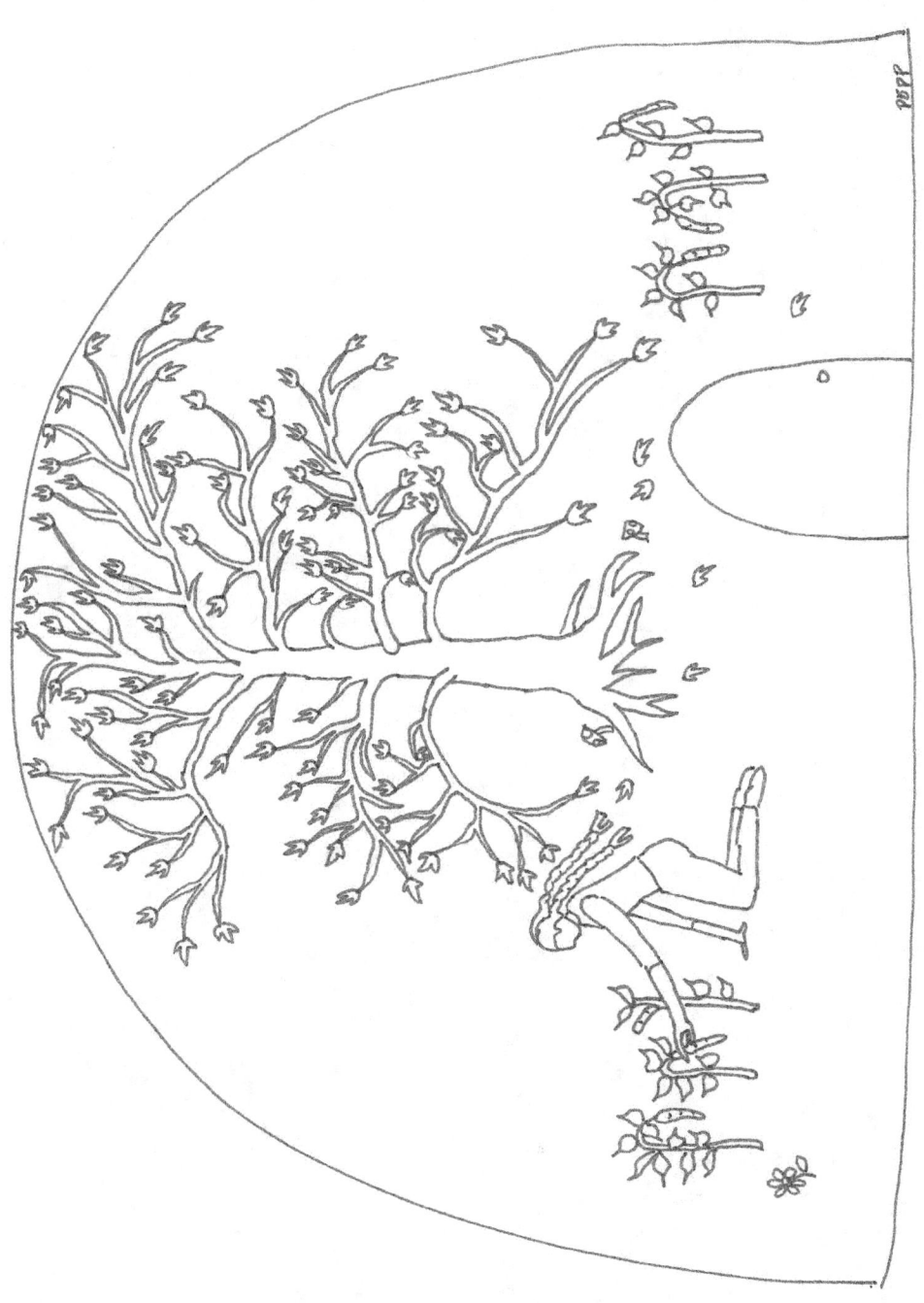

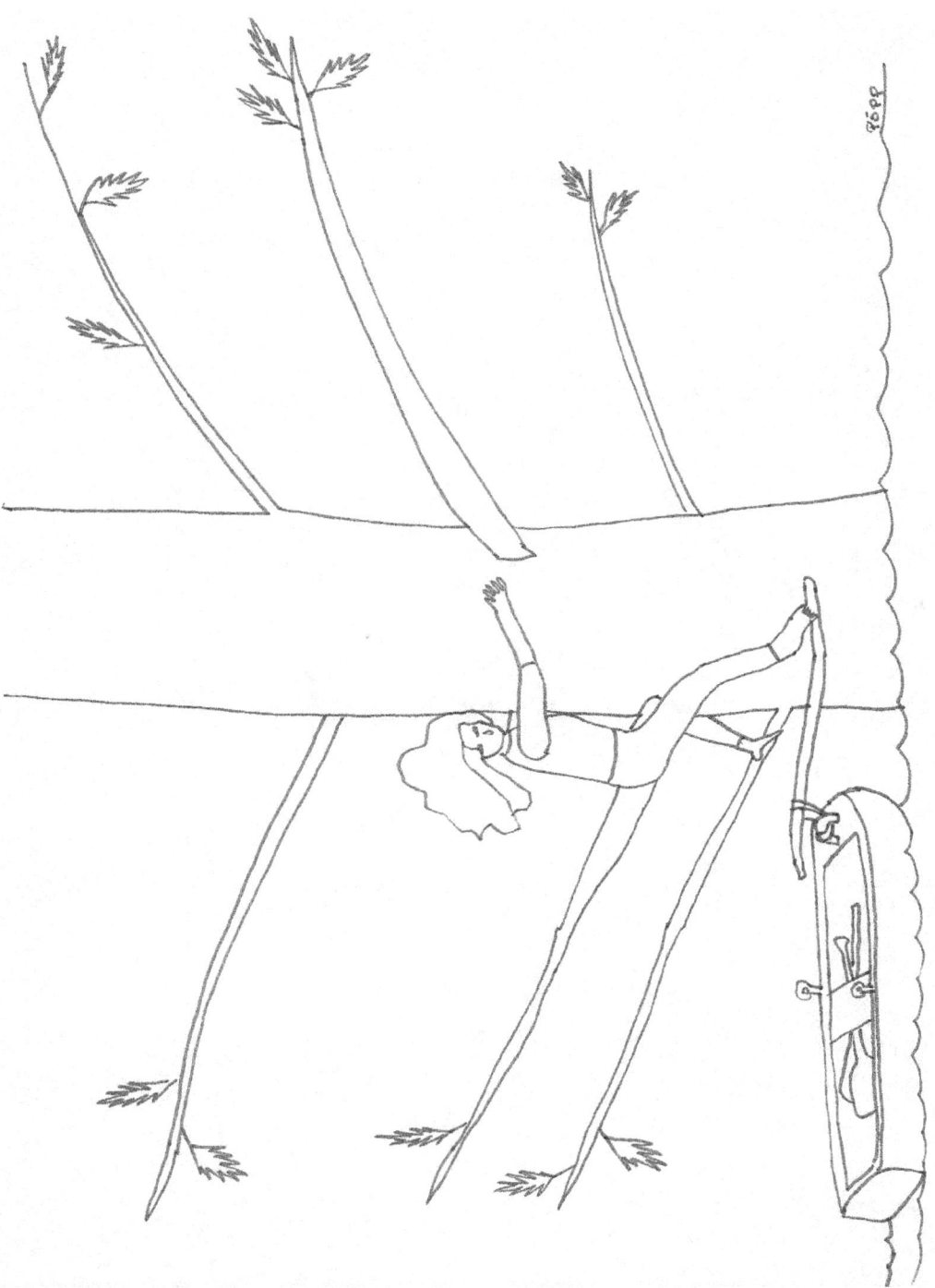

www.ingramcontent.com/pod-product-compliance
Lightning Source LLC
Chambersburg PA
CBHW081307180526
45170CB00007B/2608